Ten Minutes in Heaven

Ten Ten Minute Plays on Sex, Crime, Murder, Suicide, Satan and the Actors from the Wizard of Oz.

by Ben Ditmars

For Whitney, who brought these plays to life.

Contents

HOT SEX

<u>CHARACTERS</u>

JAKE
DEVON
RACHEL
JASON
CINDY
NICK

<u>SETTING</u>
A classroom before class.

[The new kid JAKE walks into a sparsely populated classroom and sits next to DEVON.]

JAKE: Hi, my name's Jake.

DEVON: I'm Devon.

JAKE: *[Whispering.]* There are A LOT of hot girls here!

DEVON: *[Laughing.]* Yeah, there are!

JAKE: *[Pointing at a girl, RACHEL two rows down.]* Is she available?

DEVON: Who, Rachel? You know it, player.

[RACHEL suddenly kisses a guy, JASON, beside her.]

JAKE: *[Noticeably louder.]* What the hell? I thought you said she was available!

DEVON: Relax, it's just a kiss.

JAKE: Where I come from that generally means something.

DEVON: Who said it didn't mean something?

JAKE: You did – I think!

DEVON: I told you to relax and not look into it. It might not mean an *exclusive* relationship but that doesn't make it meaningless.

JAKE: Is she a nympho?

DEVON: She's no different than any other girl or guy around.

JAKE: You make it sound like the most natural thing on earth.

DEVON: To us, it is.

JAKE: Us? What are you guys, some type of weird sex cult?

[People are staring now.]

DEVON: *[Taking a deep breath.]* A lot of people get hung up on boundaries. We just don't.

JAKE: What the whole town?

DEVON: The kids going here at least.

RACHEL: *[With a wry smile.]* I think this bothers him Cindy.

CINDY: What do you say? Should we do it?

RACHEL: Yes, let's!

[RACHEL and CINDY kiss passionately.]

JAKE: Wow, that doesn't bother you guys either?

DEVON: Two girls kissing? Of course not. Are you homophobic or something?

JAKE: A little.

DEVON: And you're judging us?

JAKE: Can't we just get back to the main issue?

DEVON: Which is?

JAKE: This town and all the free love. It's like the 1960s.

DEVON: It wasn't such a bad movement. Why should the state lord over matters of marriage?

JAKE: Because it's a holy union! It needs some recognition.

7

DEVON: I was just playing Devil's advocate. People get married here like everywhere else.

JAKE: So, what, you kiss each other's wives too? Don't you all get jealous?

DEVON: Why would we? We're secure in ourselves sexually.

JAKE: That doesn't answer the question. Relationships can't work with everybody kissing everybody else!

DEVON: Who says we stop at kissing?

JAKE: Wait, what!? You've all, like, you know what, with each other?

DEVON: That's a blunt way to put it, but yes.

JAKE: But that's adultery!

DEVON: Is it? Even those of us married are honest with each other about it. I think that's more honest than sneaking around.

JAKE: Still, it seems a pretty shallow way to live, not having real love.

DEVON: You think the rest of the world has true love? There's a divorce every five seconds! We share something together. If one of us wants to kiss someone we do it. If we want more we do that too.

JAKE: This is like the Twilight Zone or something. You're practically Mormon.

JASON: I am Mormon.

JAKE: That's what I figured.

JASON: First you bash people for their sexual orientation and now something else they can't help?

JAKE: I'm pretty sure you can help both of those things.

[JASON points his hand as if to speak.]

DEVON: *[Interrupting.]* Think about where you come from. People feel insecure, unwanted, unattractive. This town has none of that.

[Enter NICK.]

NICK: I have those notes you wanted, Devon.

[Hands him papers.]

DEVON: Thanks, man.

[They make out.]

JAKE: Ah, come on, right in front of me!? *[NICK chuckles and sits down.]* Don't you worry about diseases, for Christ sake!?

DEVON: We wouldn't hide that from each other. You'd be surprised how little there is of that when everyone's sexually familiar.

JAKE: I bet you all share property too and everything else.

DEVON: We aren't a commune. We're still capitalists.

JAKE: Yeah right. It's the freaking Manson family. Do these girls go out and murder for you?

DEVON: That's really offensive, man. We all own our own property. We just happen to respect one another. That's what capitalism should be. Not this mighty crush the weak bull shit.

JAKE: So Capitalism would work if we all had sex with each other?

9

DEVON: No, it would work without the jealousy, greed and killer instincts. It's not just about getting rich. The people around you matter too.

JAKE: *[Thinking.]* That doesn't sound so bad.

DEVON: It isn't.

JAKE: How do I get in on this?

DEVON: Not with that attitude.

JAKE: What, why!?

DEVON: It's not just about you – or any one person. You can't just jump into this. If a girl kissed another guy after you kissed her could you handle it?

JAKE: I think.

DEVON: No, you aren't sure and that's the problem.

JAKE: What if we kissed right now?

DEVON: Have you ever even kissed a guy?

JAKE: No, but I got to start somewhere!

   [They kiss.]

End of play

MACINTOSH

CHARACTERS
DON MACINTOSH: Middle-aged, worried looking man with a bad comb over.
ANN MACINTOSH: Woman in her '40s with long, red hair down to her waist; still very beautiful.

SETTING
A bedroom of mediocre furnishing. An alarm clock sits on a table with a lamp near a bed with a man and woman kissing on it.

PROPS
A small yellow bottle (for pills)
A bottle of wine
Two wine glasses

[DON rubs ANN's shoulder and moves to kiss her neck.]

DON: How does that feel honey?

ANN: Wonderful.

DON: *[Kissing her neck.]* And that?

ANN: Amazing.

DON: *[Grasping her hair.]* And that?

ANN: Better than murder, baby. *[He backs away.]* Why'd you stop?

DON: Why made you say *better than murder*?

ANN: I did not.

DON: Yes, yes, you did!

ANN: I guess I did. *[Don shrugs and goes back to kissing her. It lasts about ten seconds before ANN stops him.]* Wait, I just made an obvious allusion to murder that you don't find remotely suspicious?

DON: Should I find it remotely suspicious?

ANN: As a matter of fact… yes!

DON: *[Shocked.]* Who!?

ANN: The head of the accounting department.

DON: Your boss? But he gave us that deliciously mediocre bottle of wine last Christmas!

ANN: I know, and believe me I took it into consideration before I shot him.

DON: But we don't own a gun.

12

ANN: We don't. I do.

DON: Why didn't you tell me about it?

ANN: Well, you never know for sure if things are going to work out...

DON: Ann! For God sakes! You could go to prison!

ANN: I thought of that.

DON: And!?

ANN: That's why I killed his secretary.

DON: What!?

ANN: She knew too much. I had to tie up any loose ends, you know?

DON: No, I don't.

ANN: Relax. *[She reaches inside a bedside drawer and pulls out a bottle of wine.]* A little drink will make things better.

DON: Why did you do it?

ANN: He was working my last nerve. And I wanted a promotion. He just happened to hold the job I wanted. *[She pours DON wine, and then herself.]* Cheers?

DON: Sorry, I can't toast to premeditated slaughter.

ANN: Would a crime of passion have been any better?

DON: Very much so. When I- I mean someone- might- do it –

ANN: Don, sweet Don. I have a feeling there's blood on your hands too.

DON: Don't you see what we're becoming? Murder just leads to more murder!

ANN: More murder, eh? It sounds like it's more serious than I thought.

DON: At least I didn't kill a secretary, just my boss and our neighbor... Lily.

ANN: *[Aghast.]* Sweet, old Lily!?

DON: She saw me unloading the body. It was completely necessary. I was saving both our asses.

ANN: Only you had no idea I killed someone at the time.

DON: No... I did not.

ANN: Why did *you* do it?

DON: *[Under his breath.]* My boss? He... asked me to, uh, make him a copy.

ANN: Louder, please!

DON: HE ASKED ME TO MAKE HIM A GODDAMN COPY, SO I STABBED HIM WITH A PEN IN THE JUGULAR! *[Pause.]* Then I waited 'til the building cleared out and lifted his body into the dumpster. Happy, now?

ANN: *[Solemnly.]* Over a copy, huh? That sounds *real* irritating. At least I had a solid reason.

DON: But, can't you see, that just makes it worse?

ANN: And you had no ambition to take over your own department?

14

DON: Well… not entirely… it may have just… crossed my mind once or twice.

ANN: And after all that labeling me this and that. You should own up to it.

DON: And be proud like you?

ANN: Why not? What's done is done. *[Silence.]* Might I ask where Lily saw you taking out the body?

DON: I was going to bury it – I mean him – in the backyard.

ANN: The backyard?

DON: Yeah, I thought it was a good idea to keep the evidence as close as possible.

ANN: Amateurish. I tossed mine in the lake. Washes *away* the evidence.

DON: But it takes it out of your control. They still might find *something*.

ANN: Yeah but the corpse is miles away from you by then. *[ANN and DON suddenly start kissing again.]* Wait, wait… I think a coworker might have seen me loading the receptionist's body into the minivan.

DON: Which one? Errol, Melville!?

ANN: Melville. Definitely Melville.

DON: He put in to transfer.

ANN: We'll have to kill him before he gets the chance.

DON: I can find his address on Facebook.

ANN: I'll make sure and get some rope.

DON: You are so fucking hot right now.

ANN: I know.

DON: His home is too risky a target. Where should we get him?

ANN: Well, he leaves at five just like the rest of us. But occasionally, on Fridays he'll stay late to finish up some work and then go out for a drink. Alone.

DON: Good, good. It will be dark. Melville will likely go Willie's, the most popular and cheapest bar in town.

ANN: There's an alley he'll be walking through near the exit.

DON: I'll wait outside, wrestle him to the ground and you slit his throat.

ANN: What do we do with the body?

DON: I'll let you decide.

ANN: You're such a gentleman, Don! *[He leans in to kiss but ANN backs away.]* No... I can't. I just can't.

> *[It becomes apparent ANN is crying now.]*

DON: Why are you crying? What can't you do, Ann?

ANN: KILL! I can't keep killing.

DON: But you were so excited a moment ago.

ANN: You're right, and that's the worst part of it. I love the rush of it. But, every night I go to sleep or close my eyes I see them. I hear their screams. My hands have blood that never washes off. *[DON holds her.]* I'm sick Don. And so are you.

DON: We'll get better, Ann. You'll see. We can confess tomorrow if you want.

ANN: There's no going back now.

DON: Don't say that. There's therapy, religion, all kinds of things.

ANN: But nothing that can change what's already done. *[DON kisses her head.]* Did you hear that?

DON: No, what?

ANN: A siren. I think they're coming.

DON: Already?

ANN: Melville wouldn't waste time telling them.

DON: But this is good. We'll get the help we need sooner.

ANN: I see the victims in my head, clouding my thoughts. I can't face their families. It's too much.

DON: We'll escape then. Go to France where there's no extradition! *[Ann chuckles through her sobbing.]* What?

ANN: You're such an optimist, Don. Never lose that. *[Sirens are noticeably louder.]* Would you please do something?

DON: What?

ANN: Reach inside my purse and pull out the yellow bottle. *[DON pulls the bottle out.]* Now empty it inside my glass.

DON: What is it?

ANN: It's a very strong poison.   I had – *[Begins shaking and sobbing uncontrollably.]* Already bought for my next boss.

DON: I can't possibly do this.

ANN: Yes… you can. And somehow you'll be whole again. I know it. *[DON pours it inside her glass, weeping openly himself.]* Just one more thing now. Promise me.

DON: *[Wiping eyes.]* What?

ANN: Tell them you had nothing to do with the murders. Say it was me. *[ANN drinks the poison.]* Ah, deliciously mediocre.

   [She sets the glass on the bedside table.]

DON: But –

ANN: Don!

DON: I need prison. I need reformed. How else will I get better?

ANN: Find a new town, a new career… a new wife.

DON: I promise. The first two.

ANN: You can't cling to me. I'll kill you. Just slower than I did the others. And I can't have it happen.

DON: Wouldn't it be easier if I just drank the poison too? We could go down together like Romeo and Juliet.

ANN: That… was a tragic mistake. This is different. I know I can save you.

DON: Why the hell am I so special? Why couldn't I just die instead?

ANN: Because. You've killed. But the killing hasn't killed you yet.

DON: How do you know? I could blow away the entire office tomorrow.

ANN: But you won't. There's too much left in your heart that cares. That's good.

DON: I promise… all three.

ANN: Good. I love you Don.

DON: I love you Ann.

   [Silence.]

ANN: Do you think I'll go to hell?

DON: I – no. Jesus said many things. Blessed are the poor in spirit, blessed are the meek.

ANN: But I doubt any of that absolves me now. It looks like I'm damned to burn… alone.

DON: I'll follow you to hell then and we'll burn together and Satan himself won't come between us.

ANN: I think… I'll take that image to the grave with me.

   [Blackout as DON kisses ANN one last time.]

End of play

JUMPER

<u>CHARACTERS</u>

TIMOTHY DOBSON: Suicidal college student; melancholy with a martyr complex.

EDGAR ALLAN POE: Intellectual and well dressed. Sees macabre meaning to almost everything.

VINCENT VAN GOGH: Harsh spoken and blunt; has paint on his clothes.

EVE WEIS: Petite brunette, somewhat mousy and unsure of herself.

<u>SETTING</u>

A typical dorm room with a window. Posters hang on the wall near a dresser, a table and a lamp. Dirty clothes cover the floor.

[TIMOTHY DOBSON climbs up to the window ledge and begins a terribly rehearsed sounding monologue.]

TIMOTHY: Oh, cruel world. Has fate really brought me down to this? I was flying so high like a bird and then – shot down in my prime. Must it really end like this? I guess… it shall! *[He takes a deep breath and moves to jump; a figure, EDGAR ALLAN POE, sprints up from the side and pulls him to the floor.]* Who is this that pulls me down… down… down?

EDGAR ALLAN POE: It is I, Edgar Allan Poe. And you can desist with the classical dialogue. It is much more my foray than a mere angsty adolescent's.

TIMOTHY: *[Getting up.]* Edgar… Allan… Poe. I read you in English 356 with Professor Jones!

POE: My claim to fame as it were.

TIMOTHY: I'm like honored and all but why are you here? I had read you died in the back of a library book. So shouldn't you be like, you know, buried?

POE: The body is, of course but the spirit lingers on to help those in distress and need. So tell me what demons from the blackest night have driven you thus far?

[He pulls up a chair and crosses his legs intrigued.]

TIMOTHY: *[Nervously.]* Well… my girlfriend um… dumped me.

POE: And?

TIMOTHY: She said she loved me but she wasn't in love with me.

POE: And?

TIMOTHY: It really hurt.

POE: Did she perhaps rip out your heart and stash it underneath the floor board, where it beat driving her unto a mad confession?

TIMOTHY: No but I loved that story. The Tell-Tale something or another?

POE: Heart! I literally just said *heart*! Vincent, get out here. *[Enter a haggard looking paint-splotched man.]* This boy wants to kill himself!

VINCENT VAN GOGH: Is his life beyond repair?

POE: Not at all. His girlfriend *loves him but is not in love with him.*

VINCENT: As I've said, boyhood and youth are full of such vanity. Should it not be our ambition to become men?

TIMOTHY: Stop it! It's very serious!

VINCENT: My one true love, my soul mate art was taken from me when my brother got married and cut me off financially. Painting, apart from preaching, was all I had ever aspired or worked toward. I had nothing so I shot myself. But I'm sure your breakup was... traumatic.

TIMOTHY: Well, it was, you know, um –

POE: My wife, still young, died of tuberculosis and I drank myself to death.

TIMOTHY: Wow, you two have some real issues!

POE: But the question is: do you?

TIMOTHY: Okay, I'll tell you a little more about what happened. I'm sure you'll agree it's pretty significant. *[Pause.]* I had been going steady with this girl Eve. Things were going well but I wasn't sure if she was the one so I started seeing this other girl, Sarah, on the side.

VINCENT: On the side?

TIMOTHY: Yeah, in addition to.

POE: It sounds an affront to true and decent love.

TIMOTHY: Well it was easier than telling Eve. She might have got mad.

VINCENT: *[Matter-of-factly.]* They said I was mad.

TIMOTHY: No, not like crazy mad; angry mad.

POE: I don't follow.

TIMOTHY: Just listen! I dated Sarah a couple times and decided I still liked Eve but Eve had already found out about Sarah through a girlfriend–

VINCENT: *[Interrupting.]* A what?

TIMOTHY: Sometimes boys call their dates girlfriends but so do girls to other girls. It's like a closeness thing or something. I don't know for sure.

VINCENT: I have been gone a long time.

TIMOTHY: Like I was saying. Eve had found out about the dates with Sarah so she decided she wasn't *in love* with me and dumped me.

POE: You call that a story?

TIMOTHY: It's true! It's not a story.

POE: Obviously. The idea is to go for a single and total psychological or spiritual effect upon the reader, or in my case, the listener. Now, try again! Let's hear it!

TIMOTHY: *[Drawn out.]* Uh...

VINCENT: Edgar, I don't think this is helping the boy. Timothy, you should know that the ledge is not the answer. You've put your heart and soul into this girl and lost your very mind in the process.

TIMOTHY: What do you mean?

VINCENT: You can't think your life is over; nothing is so certain. The sight of the stars still makes you dream, does it not?

TIMOTHY: *[Looking up towards the sky from the window.]* I guess it does.

POE: The most pure, elating pleasure is the contemplation of the beautiful. I think you've been lost in that for quite some time.

TIMOTHY: But who will take me now? Everybody hates me! Even Sarah!

VINCENT: I was called the redheaded madman and cast out of my very house by petition! Acceptance is a long and winding road, you see. These things often–

TIMOTHY: *[Interrupting teary eyed.]* You can't relate to me. You lived a hundred years ago!

POE: Some things just don't change. Being young will always seem hard and indescribable to those far older and wiser. Experience, true philosophy shows truth arising from the irrelevant.

TIMOTHY: *[Angry.]* Just leave!

VINCENT: Edgar, you're coming off cold and analytical again.

POE: And you use pointless life metaphors with abandon! I was the master of 19th Century emotion!

VINCENT: *[Snappy.]* And now it's the 21st Century so give it a rest. *[Exit POE in a huff.]* Now, that he's gone perhaps we can figure things out.

TIMOTHY: I don't want talked to like a child. I had eighteen years of that at home!

VINCENT: Understandable. I went to preach the gospel in Belgium for not too dissimilar reasons.

TIMOTHY: It's not just Eve that bothers me. It's been a combination of a lot of stuff.

VINCENT: *[Reassuringly.]* There's no rush. Take your time.

TIMOTHY: *[Pausing to gather his thoughts.]* It's been really hard living on my own; doing my own laundry, getting up on time. Eve felt like someone I could talk to about it all.

VINCENT: And you felt adrift when you she left you?

TIMOTHY: Yeah, like all the things beneath the surface started creeping up.

VINCENT: Like with I and Sien. She later drowned herself, years after my death.

TIMOTHY: Do you think I hurt Eve?

VINCENT: It's not impossible. You have sat here this whole time considering how the break up affected you and you alone.

TIMOTHY: Is she okay?

VINCENT: How would I know?

TIMOTHY: You're a spirit!

VINCENT: But not a telegraph!

TIMOTHY: Telegraph?

VINCENT: They were getting quite big when I was living.

TIMOTHY: I'm going to check on her!

   [Enter Poe.]

POE: Is everything okay? I think I've thought of more to say…
through a story. You see there's this raven that flies in through the –
[TIMOTHY pushes POE out of the way and runs off stage.] Owe,
what's up with him?

VINCENT: What do you think? Things are obviously going
according to plan.

POE: Right. We might save two lives tonight instead of one.

VINCENT: It's better to make mistakes high spirited than be
narrow-minded and prudent. Come on.

   [Exit POE and VINCENT together.

   Lights fade and return to reveal TIMOTHY and EVE.]

EVE: I'm glad you found me. I don't know what I might've done if
you hadn't.

TIMOTHY: Let's not think about it right now.

EVE: I was so hurt and confused, you know? I knew you were right
for me in so many ways but I just couldn't picture myself being with
someone…

TIMOTHY: Unfaithful?

EVE: Yeah.

TIMOTHY: But I can change. I was just going through a lot.

EVE: And I wasn't? I had a new home and new life to get used to too, you know. You think college and a part time job isn't stressful?

TIMOTHY: I'm sorry Eve. For everything. I didn't know what I had in you until it wasn't there.

EVE: That's reassuring. I'm so bland and unimportant you couldn't tell?

TIMOTHY: No, nothing like that! It's just...

EVE: What?

TIMOTHY: I didn't want to be like them.

EVE: Who?

TIMOTHY: My parents. Married young and always fighting, passing all their problems off on me.

EVE: That's a stupid reason to think I'm not *the one*. By that logic no one would ever be! And you'd be alone forever!

TIMOTHY: Sometimes I thought that was better.

EVE: It isn't. You don't have to be your father just like I don't have to be my mother. We're different people! And we can have a normal relationship and normal children someday.

TIMOTHY: But what if we don't?

EVE: You can't let fear dictate your life. Trust yourself, trust me for a change!

TIMOTHY: I'll try. Because I know you're worth it. *[Pause.]* Give me another chance?

EVE: I guess I have to. You saw what I'm like without you.

> [TIMOTHY and EVE continue talking as it turns to mostly silent gesturing.]

POE: [Offstage.] Not exactly a fairy tale ending, Vincent.

VINCENT: [Offstage.] We did the best we could.

POE: [Offstage.] If I weren't dead it might make a nice poem.

VINCENT: [Offstage.] Or interesting painting? I could paint them stars in the night sky.

POE: [Offstage.] It's getting late. I must be getting back to Virginia. We're having dinner with Thoreau. You're welcome to join us.

VINCENT: [Offstage.] As always, I will try. However, the heavenly landscape is a tempting subject to not gaze upon.

TIMOTHY: They think we can't hear them.

EVE: Childish but sweet.

> [Lights fade as TIMOTHY and EVE exit holding hands.]

End of play

BANK ROB

CHARACTERS

MR. MATHEWS: Shabby looking older man.
FRANK: Slick robber in his late-twenties.
BOSS: Balding, stocky, officious type in charge of the operation.

SETTING
A run of the mill bank with loan offices in back and a line of patrons waiting for service from the tellers.

PROPS
A plastic bag
Three handguns

[FRANK, steps in front of a loan office and pulls out a gun. He approaches an ambivalent customer, MR. MATHEWS.]

FRANK: Put your wallet in the bag! *[MR. MATHEWS stares blankly.]* Put it in the bag or I'll fucking shoot you!

MR. MATHEWS: Go ahead, I have nothing to live for.

FRANK: What?

MR. MATHEWS: Shoot, please. I have no family left to bother you.

FRANK: This is depressing. I'm gonna, uh, talk to the boss. *[He walks over to, BOSS, a man counting money.]* Boss, this guy doesn't care if I shoot him.

BOSS: Why would someone not care? He's bluffing. Fire in the air once or twice and he'll cooperate.

FRANK: Won't that ruin the ceiling?

BOSS: *[Rolling eyes.]* You're a burglar for God sakes. Grow a pair!

[FRANK walks back to MR. MATHEWS.]

FRANK: Okay, no more sad stories.

[Fires gun into the air.]

MR. MATHEWS: I think you aimed too high. Try a little lower next time. *[FRANK fires into the air once more.]* Why did you shoot the ceiling again?

FRANK: Boss said do it twice. Be right back.

[FRANK walks back to BOSS.]

BOSS: What now!?

FRANK: He doesn't care.

BOSS: Make him!

FRANK: I fired my gun in the air. Everyone else seemed plenty scared.

BOSS: Don't let anyone be a goddamn hero, Frank. You know better.

FRANK: I don't think he's a hero. He's just very dissatisfied with the direction his life has taken. There might be a recent loss or latent trauma affecting him. *[BOSS gives FRANK a quizzical look.]* I majored in psychology.

BOSS: I don't care if you majored in Herbology with Professor fucking McGonagall!

FRANK: Actually, it was Professor Sprout and Neville... in the epilogue.

> *[BOSS slaps FRANK upside the head.]*

BOSS: Get over there and take care of things before anyone else gets similar ideas!

> *[FRANK walks back and whispers into MR. MATHEWS' ear.]*

FRANK: I'm, uh, sorry for your recent loss.

MR. MATHEWS: What loss?

FRANK: Don't worry. I get not wanting to talk things over so publicly.

MR. MATHEWS: Honestly, I haven't had any family for going on twenty years.

FRANK: Maybe you have Post Traumatic Stress Disorder from a war?

MR. MATHEWS: No, no, nothing of the sort.

FRANK: Then put your money in the fucking bag!

MR. MATHEWS: Not until you fucking shoot me!

FRANK: *[Cocking pistol.]* FINE!

MR. MATHEWS: That's more like it.

　　　　[FRANK fires hitting MR. MATHEWS in the arm.]

FRANK: Holy shit, what have I done!?

MR. MATHEWS: *[Falling to the ground.]* Obviously, not enough!

　　　　[FRANK runs to BOSS.]

FRANK: I shot him!

BOSS: You, what!?

FRANK: I shot him.

BOSS: I said take care of things, not take care of *him.*

FRANK: What do I do?

BOSS: Find a bandage and wrap him up before he bleeds to death. We don't murder, Frank.

FRANK: We're criminals, though. Doesn't that come with the name?

BOSS: No more than committing genocide comes with the title of president. You always have a choice in who you are, if not what. Now, go help that man before he dies!

FRANK: Okay.

[He returns to MR. MATHEWS.]

MR. MATHEWS: You're back. Are you gonna kill me or what?

FRANK: *[Ripping his shirt sleeve off and making a bandage.]* No. I'm going to save you.

MR. MATHEWS: Why?

FRANK: Because no one else will. *[Pause.]* But, tell me, why are you so dead set on dying, if you don't mind my pun?

MR. MATHEWS: I've told you. I have no one.

FRANK: Then find someone.

MR. MATHEWS: People always give those sorts of answers. Oh, you live in a bad place, just move. Oh, he abuses you, just leave. It's never that simple.

FRANK: It was for me.

MR. MATHEWS: What do you mean?

FRANK: I hated my job. I had just gotten out of college, felt my life had no direction. Then, I got into this. I feel important, alive, you know? No, you don't know. But I think you can.

MR. MATHEWS: Clearly I'm not you.

FRANK: But why not?

MR. MATHEWS: You can find another job because it's solely dependent on yourself. Finding another person is dependent on other people as well. I can't make people enjoy my company.

FRANK: You can't?

MR. MATHEWS: Of course not.

FRANK: Maybe you're just not letting people see the real you.

MR. MATHEWS: Like I haven't heard the therapists say that before.

FRANK: Hold my gun.

MR. MATHEWS: That I've never heard.

FRANK: *[Handing him a gun.]* Take it. *[MR. MATHEWS takes the gun with his good arm.]* How does it feel?

MR. MATHEWS: Heavy.

FRANK: No, I mean, how does it *feel*? Like inside.

MR. MATHEWS: Well, I kind of wanna shoot something.

FRANK: Go ahead.

MR. MATHEWS: You're crazy. I'll murder someone.

FRANK: Shoot where I shot in the ceiling. If anyone asks it was me. *[MR. MATHEWS takes FRANK's gun and fires up in the air.]* Nice shot. I think you hit the sprinklers though.

MR. MATHEWS: That was a terrible idea.

FRANK: Of course it was but how does it feel?

MR. MATHEWS: Kind of sickening. I'm shaking all over from the sprinkler water.

FRANK: But, do you feel, motivated, alive?

MR. MATHEWS: I suppose there's a small part of me that might say that.

FRANK: Then good. You can join us.

MR. MATHEWS: What!?

FRANK: Rob banks with us.

MR. MATHEWS: I'm not a criminal. I'm just an average citizen.

FRANK: Sure.

MR. MATHEWS: What do you mean by that?

FRANK: You're not a citizen at all, you're a ghost that fades into the background. Join us and do something invigorating. Make your life memorable. Make it count for something.

MR. MATHEWS: But stealing is… wrong!

FRANK: Stealing your life away is wrong. You need this and the world needs a hero.

MR. MATHEWS: Okay, now, you're exaggerating. You think you're a hero stealing the money of innocent people?

FRANK: Did you ever stop to think what we do with the money we steal?

MR. MATHEWS: No but normally gangsters and thugs would use it for narcotics.

FRANK: We give nearly ninety-nine percent of it away.

MR. MATHEWS: Sure you do.

FRANK: Large donations to charitable organizations aren't deemed suspicious by the feds.

MR. MATHEWS: Okay, name five charities you've given to.

FRANK: The American Cancer Society, the Red Cross, St. Jude Children's Hospital, Meals on Wheels and most recently, the Muscular Dystrophy Association.

MR. MATHEWS: Name five more.

FRANK: *[Taking breath.]* The Sierra Club, the ACLU, Doctors Without Borders, Save the Children and Bhopal Medical Appeal.

MR. MATHEWS: All right, you're good but tell me what one of those organizations actually does.

FRANK: The Bhopal Medical Appeal helps the victims of the Union Carbide disaster in Bhopal, India, one of the worst on record. They invest in healthcare for those dealing with the fallout.

MR. MATHEWS: I never thought I'd say this but, yeah. Sign me up.

FRANK: Just keep that gun and follow me. Mind your arm.

[MR. MATHEWS follows FRANK.]

BOSS: Did you fix up his arm up or what?

FRANK: Yeah, but there's another thing now. I asked him to join us.

BOSS: Why for God sakes?

FRANK: He needs us.

BOSS: We may give to charity, but we are *not* a charity! Do you know anything about this man? He could be a goddamned pig!

FRANK: He isn't. I have a feeling.

BOSS: Oh, well when we're all in prison I can take comfort in your *feeling*.

FRANK: You said to help that man *[Points to MR. MATHEWS.]* before he dies. That is precisely what I'm doing.

BOSS: Frank, just ask yourself; is this man's happiness equal to all the children and sick individuals we'd be helping if we stayed out of prison? I ask you to remember what really happened after college. If you can go back to that and still want this potential cop on the team, I'll go along with it.

MR. MATHEWS: What does he mean?

FRANK: Nothing. Go back and sit down.

MR. MATHEWS: *[Pointing gun.]* No, tell me, now.

FRANK: You don't know how to aim that thing. *[MR. MATHEWS cocks pistol.]* Or maybe you do.

MR. MATHEWS: Like I said, tell me.

FRANK: Are you a cop?

MR. MATHEWS: No, I'm FBI.

FRANK: But, I defended you. Was anything you said true?

MR. MATHEWS: I had a cover story. Now, get on the ground. The building will soon be surrounded. It's over.

FRANK: But doesn't charity mean something to you? We're helping people!

MR. MATHEWS: No, you've just made them liable, if it's even true.

BOSS: You should have trusted me.

FRANK: Yeah.

BOSS: Now there's only one option.

FRANK: Yeah.

> *[BOSS slips a spare pistol to FRANK.]*

> *They both shoot MR.MATHEWS.]*

BOSS: He didn't have the guts to fire first.

FRANK: I suppose not.

BOSS: But, now you gotta say out loud what really got you into this before we escape.

FRANK: Do I have–

BOSS: Frank!

FRANK: I got in a bad place with my debt… and turned to the mob.

BOSS: And who saved your ass?

FRANK: You did.

BOSS: Remember that.

FRANK: Looks like we're just about surrounded outside.

BOSS: I say we make a run for it.

FRANK: Are you sure?

BOSS: Have I steered you wrong before?

[Lights fade as BOSS and FRANK run offstage to the sound of bullets.]

End of play

PIRATES OF THE OLENTANGY RIVER

CHARACTERS

BLACK RACER SNAKE (GRETCHEN BRANDT): The captain. Nine years old and most knowledgeable about pirates.

SCIOTO SAMMIE (SAMANTHA DAVIS): The first mate. Stout, large middle-aged woman. Quick to anger and not one to cross.

BUCKEYE BART (BARTHOLOMEW TAYLOR): Boatswain. An overweight male in his late thirties wearing an Ohio State jersey and a necklace of buckeye nuts.

BURGER BEARD (ZACHARY MEADE): Powder monkey. Terribly obese, putting even Bart to shame. He loves to eat and does so constantly.

LONG TOM SALVIA (THOMAS WHITE): Gunner. Thin, tall, balding with a large mustache. His name is not clever; he is terribly addicted to salvia

SETTING

A motorboat; somewhere between Delaware and Powell.

PROPS

A Barbie Doll
Several sandwiches

[BLACK RACER SNAKE is at the bow, with SCIOTO SAMMIE, BUCKEYE BART, BURGER BEARD and LONG TOM SALVIA behind.]

BLACK RACER SNAKE: Man that throttle, Buckeye Bart! Sammie, cut across the waves at no less than a 45 degree angle and stay perpendicular! Don't forget to watch for bogies on our tail, Long Tom! Burger Beard, put down that Egg McMuffin!

BUCKEYE BART: What will you be doing?

BLACK RACER SNAKE: I'm nine years old. I suspect I'll be playing with Barbies or something.

BUCKEYE BART: And *she's* our captain!

SCIOTO SAMMIE: *[Pushing BART.]* Don't you dare say another word against the captain!

BUCKEYE BART: Your first mate can't defend you forever.

BLACK RACER SNAKE: She doesn't have to!

[BLACK RACER SNAKE reaches back and punches BART in the groin.]

BART: *[In terrible impersonation of a real pirate.]* Me clams!

[He passes out on BURGER BEARD.]

SCIOTO SAMMIE: Does anyone else have something to say?

BURGER BEARD: *[Raising hand.]* I do.

SCIOTO SAMMIE: And what is that?

BURGER BEARD: *[Still eating an Egg McMuffin.]* What's for lunch?

41

BLACK RACER SNAKE: Burger Beard, honestly, you still haven't finished breakfast!

BURGER BEARD: But it's almost gone!

BLACK RACER SNAKE: We'll stop for port sometime in the next few hours. Have lunch then!

BURGER BEARD: It will be too late! We'll need dinner!

BLACK RACER SNAKE: First mate, whip this yellow belly into shape!

SCIOTO SAMMIE: Listen to the captain you scurvy wolverine! Pick up those bullets. You'll hand them to Long Tom when he needs 'em. It's all you're good for anyway!

LONG TOM SALVIA: There's never nothin' to shoot! Except those flying crocodiles I keep spotting…

SCIOTO SAMMIE: Damn it, Tom, are you still on the salvia?

LONG TOM SALVIA: I'm on a lot of things… in a lot of places.

SCIOTO SAMMIE: It literally scares the shit out of me you're our gunner.

BLACK RACER SNAKE: *[Playing with Barbie dolls.]* No cursing!

BUCKEYE BART: *[With a mischievous smile.]* Perhaps I could be the gunner?

SCIOTO SAMMIE: It's far too obvious you're planning mutiny…

BLACK RACER SNAKE: Could you all quiet down, I'm trying to assemble a dream house over here.

BUCKEYE BART: You don't have a dream house!

42

BLACK RACER SNAKE: It's called *imagination*, stupid.

BUCKEYE BART: I don't see why I'm not the captain. I'm the oldest and a *man*!

SCIOTO SAMMI: Okay, then genius, what do you know about the waters?

BUCKEYE BART: Well, occasionally there's bridges. We should, um, be careful with those?

SCIOTO SAMMIE: Gretchen, show him what you know.

BLACK RACER SNAKE: I attended the overnight program on the replica of the Santa Maria as well as the festivities with goodybags and pirate hats. I'm versed in the ways of the 15th Century sailor. I know what it takes to survive and you will listen, or you will walk the plank. Got it?

BUCKEYE BART: *[Meekly.]* Yes.

BLACK RACER SNAKE: Good. Now, let's follow that heading… *[Looks at compass.]* North!

BURGER BEARD: Aye!

SCIOTO SAMMIE: Captain, where exactly are we headed by the way?

BLACK RACER SNAKE: To treasure of course!

SCIOTO SAMMIE: But which treasure? I can't imagine there's much on the shores of the Olentangy.

BLACK RACER SNAKE: True, it is not of the buried variety. But there is a Joe's Crab Shack not far inland.

BUCKEYE BART: You suggest we rob… a Joe's!?

43

BLACK RACER SNAKE: Why not? We can easily make a getaway into the boat, and they'll think we're just another fishing group.

SCIOTO SAMMIE: Won't the stolen crab cakes and money give us away?

BLACK RACER SNAKE: That's why we eat the food and bury the cash, like pirates!

LONG TOM SALVIA: I'm going to need more salvia.

SCIOTO SAMMIE: This is a bit more dangerous than I imagined, Gretch. I thought we'd just be digging for discarded quarters, maybe pilfering some old boats.

BLACK RACER SNAKE: Don't you remember why you all signed up in the first place?

SCIOTO SAMMIE: Of course, we do. They cut my hours back at Whirlpool. I needed something to support my kids.

BURGER BEARD: I got fired for eating too many doubles at Wendy's.

LONG TOM SALVIA: I lost my job at the convenience store.

BLACK RACER SNAKE: And I lost my paper route. See what the system's done to us? It's time to take something back for once!

SCIOTO SAMMIE: All right, Gretchen, we're with you.

BLACK RACER SNAKE: Good. Now let's go over the plan!

SCIOTO SAMMIE: Okay, what is it?

BLACK RACER SNAKE: I was hoping one of you might have some ideas.

LONG TOM SALVIA: We could go in there like riding dragons and steal Gringott's gold.

BLACK RACER SNAKE: That's not canon to the Harry Potter books and you know it!

LONG TOM SALVIA: *[Apologetically.]* Sorry.

BLACK RACER SNAKE: Come on, ideas people!

SCIOTO SAMMIE: We must examine Joe's weaknesses.

BLACK RACER SNAKE: Good, what are they?

BURGER BEARD: Their crab legs are overpriced!

BUCKEYE BART: Since when have you ever gotten a good deal on crab legs anywhere, Zach? They're always overpriced.

BURGER BEARD: Not true. I got a great deal down in Florida once.

BLACK RACER SNAKE: Coming back to the point; how do we pull off the heist?

BURGER BEARD: We'll pose as employees. I sometimes do it to get free biscuits.

BLACK RACER SNAKE: It's a good idea but it's not very *piratey*.

BURGER BEARD: What's more piratey than free food? Do you suggest we go in guns blazing?

BLACK RACER SNAKE: I would but we only have the one gun.

BURGER BEARD: So gun blazing?

BLACK RACER SNAKE: If Tom thinks he's up to it…

LONG TOM SALVIA: I don't, I really don't.

BLACK RACER SNAKE: There's more to being a pirate than doing salvia, Tom.

LONG TOM SALVIA: Maybe to you.

SCIOTO SAMMIE: You'll do it or else!

LONG TOM SALVIA: Or else what? *[SCIOTO SAMMIE grasps his collar.]* Okay. If you're gonna be like that…

SCIOTO SAMMIE: She's all yours captain!

BLACK RACER SNAKE: Thanks Sam. There's much booty in this for you! *[LONG TOM SALVIA chuckles.]* Tom, how old are you?

LONG TOM SALVIA: Twenty-seven.

BLACK RACER SNAKE: That was rhetorical.

LONG TOM SALVIA: Rhetorical?

BLACK RACER SNAKE: *[Fed up.]* Never mind.

BUCKEYE BART: Are you sure we're headed the right way?

SCIOTO SAMMIE: Why so anxious?

BUCKEYE BART: *[Evasively.]* No reason.

BURGER BEARD: I think he's holding something back.

SCIOTO SAMMIE: Like what?

BLACK RACER SNAKE: He's alerted the authorities.

BUCKEYE BART: How did you–

BLACK RACER SNAKE: Know? Please, Bart. You couldn't have been more transparent.

SCIOTO SAMMIE: Why did you wait until now to mention it!? Scurvy wolverine! I would have made him walk the plank!

BLACK RACER SNAKE: That's precisely why. I had to give him the benefit of the doubt.

> *[Silence.]*

SCIOTO SAMMI: So what do we do now?

> *[Crew is fidgety and nervous now; BUCKEYE BART is hanging his head; LONG TOM is not concentrated on his salvia for once; BURGER beard eats faster.]*

BLACK RACER SNAKE: There's land ahead.

SCIOTO SAMMIE: It's lit up with police lights! I can see them from here! Captain, why on Earth didn't you take another course?

BLACK RACER SNAKE: Like I said, I had to know for sure.

LONG TOM SALVIA: But we haven't committed any crimes!

BLACK RACER SNAKE: It doesn't matter, they'll get us for conspiracy post 9/11.

> *[SCIOTO SAMMIE starts pushing BUCKEYE BART again.]*

BLACK RACER SNAKE: Sammie, stop!

SCIOTO SAMMIE: Why? He's ruined us! I'll throw him off without any of your help!

BUCKEYE BART: I couldn't sail under a nine year old, anymore. I had to take charge and be a man!

47

SCIOTO SAMMIE: They'll arrest you too, dumb ass!

BUCKEYE BART: No, that was part of the deal. I get to keep the boat.

SCIOTO SAMMIE: You are so far from a man right now, Bart. A man puts his friends and family first. A man has balls. You're as flat as Gretchen's Ken doll where it counts!

BUCKEYE BART: But at least I'll have the boat.

SCIOTO SAMMIE: It's going into evidence. The most they'll leave you with is cowardice.

[BUCKEYE BART looks to BLACK RACER SNAKE.]

BLACK RACER SNAKE: This was all pretty despicable Bart.

BUCKEYE BART: What do you know? You're nine! I've never had a thing in my life and for once I finally will.

BLACK RACER SNAKE: I hope it brings you comfort. I really do.

BURGER BEARD: Any further instructions captain?

BLACK RACER SNAKE: Courage. We'll all need plenty.

End of play

DUMPSTER BOOGIE

[JOHN approaches a dumpster and looks inside.]

JOHN: Excuse me, do you live in here?

[A disheveled form, OSCAR, pops his head out.]

OSCAR: No, I'm visiting with an empty can of tuna fish – of course I live here!

JOHN: I hate to be a bother but, I'm recently homeless and was wondering… can I crash here for tonight?

OSCAR: Actually, I would. Very much. It's crowded as is.

JOHN: You don't own the dumpster!

OSCAR: No but I'll sure as hell fight for it!

JOHN: Well, looking at me and looking at you I think it's a battle I might win.

OSCAR: I have home field advantage. There's broken bottles, sharp can lids… any number of things that I'd find first.

JOHN: So, wouldn't it be polite to give me something sharp as well?

OSCAR: I suppose, if the streets were polite. But they aren't. So fuck off and find a park bench!

JOHN: Didn't anyone help you out when you first lost your home!?

[Pause.]

OSCAR: Fine. Come on in.

[JOHN climbs into the dumpster.]

JOHN: It's not so bad in here. The trash is nicely sorted, so I'm not standing in anything too gross.

OSCAR: I like to make it feel like a home as much as I can.

JOHN: *[Extending hand.]* My name's John.

OSCAR: *[Shaking.]* Mine's… Oscar.

JOHN: No, really?

OSCAR: Yes, really. You have a problem with it?

JOHN: It's just kind of ironic is all.

OSCAR: How so?

JOHN: You live in a dumpster… and your name is Oscar. Also, not to rub it in or anything, but you're kind of a grouch.

OSCAR: I fail to see the humor in all this.

JOHN: Okay, I'll let it go then. Geesh. Sorry.

   [Pause.]

OSCAR: What's your last name John?

JOHN: *[Under his breath.]* Hancock.

OSCAR: Ha. A founding father's namesake homeless. Telling sign if you ask me.

JOHN: *[Hanging head.]* I suppose so. Can't really argue the point.

OSCAR: Don't feel too bad. My surname is rather symbolic itself.

JOHN: What is it?

OSCAR: Mayer. Oscar Mayer.

JOHN: That does brighten my day considerably.

OSCAR: Well, just think of all that Oscar Mayer stands for: a giant company, producing food. And then look at me; hungry, poor with no discernable wealth whatsoever.

JOHN: If Dickens were alive he'd have a field day...

OSCAR: How did you lose your home?

JOHN: I really don't know. I worked hard my whole life; made every right decision. Look where it's gotten me.

OSCAR: But the prevailing wisdom in Washington is something *must* be wrong with you. Otherwise you'd still be successful.

JOHN: I guess I didn't work hard enough... I must be a bum.

OSCAR: *[Laughing.]* Well, we both are now!

JOHN: So why are you homeless?

OSCAR: My family was poor.

JOHN: *[Chuckling.]* But, really, why?

OSCAR: The way society is structured? I was born to the wrong parents, in the wrong neighborhood, at the wrong time. Schools were underfunded. No one helped me realize my potential. Take your pick.

JOHN: Well, I guess this is true equality then. You and I in this dumpster together.

OSCAR: The man who had it all and the man who had nothin.'

JOHN: I'd drink to that if I could still afford it.

OSCAR: There was a little left in a bottle of whiskey someone didn't drink completely. I can try to find it.

[He starts digging around the side of the dumpster.]

JOHN: Reminds me of how I was, throwing things away. I was so damned wasteful. I'd give anything to have back some of the food I tossed.

OSCAR: *[Emerging.]* I found it.

JOHN: Thank God, reality wasn't getting any easier. *[OSCAR takes a drink and hands the bottle to JOHN.]* This is glass?

OSCAR: Last I checked.

JOHN: *[To himself.]* Good, good.

[He suddenly breaks the bottle and holds the sharp edge to OSCAR's throat.]

OSCAR: What the hell are you doing!?

JOHN: What I planned to all along. The dumpster is mine now!

OSCAR: Don't do this.

JOHN: Why wouldn't I? A man has to make a profit somehow.

OSCAR: Profit?

JOHN: Disaster capitalism at its finest. I used to be high up in the derivatives market. Now I rent dumpsters.

OSCAR: You can't rent what you don't own!

JOHN: Naïve of you to think so. Many a man has made millions selling what he didn't own. Ever hear of the slave trade, land grants in the 1800s? Even my derivatives and hedge fund markets were in on it.

OSCAR: This is a fucking dumpster if you haven't noticed.

JOHN: Yes and whoever gives me the best price gets to live here.

OSCAR: What if I get out and come back to kill you later?

JOHN: I would have sold it off by then.

OSCAR: Well I'm not going to do that anyway.

JOHN: Good to hear.

OSCAR: I'm going to stay here and let you murder me.

JOHN: You act like I've never done that before.

OSCAR: You might have. But I have a feeling you're too much of a bitch.

JOHN: I wouldn't go there when a man has glass against your throat.

OSCAR: Go ahead; you think I've got anything to lose?

   [JOHN hesitates and OSCAR takes the bottle from him.]

JOHN: Fuck.

OSCAR: *[Turning the bottle over in his hands.]* Now what to do, what to do?

JOHN: Listen, Oscar, things got a little out of control is all.

OSCAR: *[Angry.]* I actually trusted you and you were nothing but a goddamn conman!

JOHN: We all do what we have to, to survive out here. You know how it is!

OSCAR: I've been poor and homeless most of my life and I don't know *how it is*. It's obviously different for you *new poor*. I should have realized. All you've ever known is comfort and profit and getting that back is all that matters to you. Another person's life doesn't mean shit. Humanity itself doesn't mean shit.

JOHN: You've pinpointed it. I'm a selfish, selfish bastard. Now just let me go, and you can have the dumpster to yourself again.

OSCAR: I would, but I'm not done with you just yet.

JOHN: No?

OSCAR: I've got a lot of different things in here that I've collected.

JOHN: What kind of things?

OSCAR: All kinds; syringes, razor blades. I think it's time we test some of them out.

JOHN: Look, I'm sorry. What do you plan on proving!?

OSCAR: When the next person sees you they'll know just the kind of person you are. *[OSCAR tackles JOH and, an unseen feud occurs where OSCAR fixes JOHN's shirt pocket.]* That should do it!

JOHN: *[Surfacing.]* I look exactly the same.

OSCAR: Just a little better though.

JOHN: Hey… you fixed my shirt pocket.

OSCAR: That I did.

JOHN: Why?

OSCAR: No one will mistake your intentions now. Welcome to the street. *[Pause.]* Now get out.

JOHN: But, I won't have anywhere else to go.

OSCAR: And yet you were willing to do the same to me.

JOHN: You're too good of a person to throw me out.

OSCAR: Wanna bet?

JOHN: Yeah, I'd bet what little I still have. I'm too much of a coward to kill you and you're too much of a coward to throw me out.

OSCAR: It would seem we're kind of stuck then. Unless I did something really stupid.

JOHN: What would that be? *[OSCAR starts rocking the dumpster.]* Stop! You'll tip it over! *[The dumpster falls over.]* Now what on earth has this accomplished?

OSCAR: Listen. Can't you hear the owners coming? We're both leaving tonight.

JOHN: If the cops arrest us there's no way I'm sharing a cell with you.

[Lights fade.]

End of play

CRASHING NOAH'S ARK

CHARACTERS

NOAH: Righteous, or at least perceives himself as such. Wears robes and traditional male biblical attire. Slightly drunk from a long voyage at sea.

EMZARA: Noah's wife. Irate and short tempered, the voyage, and her husband are beginning to wear on her. She has robes similar to Noah's.

HANK: A crafty con-man of sorts. He sports a terribly unconvincing dinosaur costume with teeth drawn on a hood and his face in plain view.

SETTING

The ark's third deck. Stairs, leading to a skylight roof, are adjacent and several different pens for animals are seen. A window is near floor level.

[NOAH is engaged in a heated argument with his wife EMZARA.]

NOAH: I was given this task, Emzara! Not you!

EMZARA: And that makes it okay to kill millions of innocent people?

NOAH: They weren't innocent! Not a one of them!

EMZARA: How are you so sure?

NOAH: God spoke to me.

EMZARA: And that automatically clears you of all discretion?

NOAH: The lord sees more than I could ever hope to.

EMZARA: Maybe he's tested you and you've already failed. *[A knock above is heard.]* What's that?

NOAH: Perhaps it's God.

EMZARA: Honestly. Just open the skylight roof already.

NOAH: But the Lord said to wait until after the fortieth day.

EMZARA: *[Sarcastically.]* Maybe he has further instructions?

NOAH: Likely. He hasn't said much lately.

> *[NOAH climbs up the ladder to the skylight roof.*
>
> *He opens it and a body falls on him.]*

EMZARA: *[From below.]* What is it?

NOAH: *[Holding a limp form.]* It's a body.

EMZARA: Are they dead?

NOAH: I'm not sure.

> *[NOAH climbs back down.*
>
> *He lays a body dressed as some type of dinosaur near the stairs.]*

EMZARA: Is he breathing?

NOAH: Yes. Just. *[HANK, the body, coughs water and suddenly leaps up.]* Wow!

HANK: *[Enthusiastically.]* Hello!

NOAH: Where have you come from?

HANK: The Jurassic age. Can't you tell? I have a tail.

NOAH: What is this *Jurassic age* of which you speak?

HANK: It's when the dinosaurs lived.

NOAH: Dinosaurs?

HANK: Yes, you don't have any on the ship, do you?

NOAH: No…

HANK: Well, that'll sure piss off the evangelicals in a few thousand years but at least there's some room. Where do I lodge?

EMZARA: You can stay with our son Shem on the first deck…

NOAH: Emzara, silence! First off, *stowaway*, your species was not on the list. Second, your tail just fell off.

HANK: Lizards, what can I say, we like to shed.

[He reattaches his tail.]

NOAH: You realize I can see a human face underneath that set of crudely drawn teeth on your hood?

HANK: My face has assumed human form as not to frighten you.

NOAH: You really expect me to believe that?

HANK: Of course. It's your duty to ensure safe passage for all creatures of the earth and sky.

NOAH: Yes, two of every kind. There's just one of you.

HANK: Maybe I'll lay an egg.

EMZARA: Let him stay!

NOAH: Emzara, stay out of this!

HANK: In my reptilian culture we treat women with a little more respect.

NOAH: One more word and I'm throwing you out!

EMZARA: He's swam the flood for forty days! God obviously wants him to live!

NOAH: God commanded me to build the ark, and to have two of every animal. He said nothing of this!

EMZARA: If you throw him out you will be no better than those the Lord has sentenced to death!

HANK: Hey, still here. *[Takes off his dinosaur hood.]* Not to butt in but there were plenty of innocent, God fearing people taken by the waters. My family, among them. *[NOAH huffs.]* What was that?

60

NOAH: You came here in an attempt to trick us. I can't help but think that reflects on the type of family life you must have had. Especially since I see you… and no family!

[HANK slaps NOAH.]

HANK: What the hell makes you so righteous?

NOAH: *[Touching the sore spot on his cheek.]* The lord chose me to live and build this ark.

HANK: Really? I think he cursed you!

EMZARA: Stop! This has gone too far.

NOAH: No… tell me, how am I cursed?

HANK: It would seem to me, if I were chosen to witness the destruction of all life on earth, it would be far from a blessing.

NOAH: Then thank Heavens you are not the Lord!

HANK: I don't think you were a righteous man, at all, Noah. Your pretense is that God thought you somehow above the others that died. I think you were, instead, a wicked man God sought to punish! Death would be better by far than your fate!

NOAH: Then why are you still alive?

HANK: I wanted at least one righteous man to survive on this earth.

[NOAH begins weeping.]

EMZARA: Noah, what's gotten into you?

NOAH: He's right. He's absolutely right. And so were you! It was a test; the ultimate test. Would I build an ark to save myself and my family knowing all other life on earth would die? And I did! I did just that Emzara! Children, fathers, mothers DEAD!

61

EMZARA: You can't be so hard on yourself. You were just following the Lord's commands as any pious man might!

NOAH: No, there is such a thing as discretion. Maybe it wasn't God speaking to me after all. It could have been Satan tempting me! I can see it now: Satan approaching God and telling him his most loyal follower would never sacrifice others for his own needs! And he was right! I've failed. It wasn't the rest of the world that was wicked. It was me!

HANK: Maybe it wasn't God or Satan. Perhaps it was just terrible coincidence.

NOAH: *[Still sobbing.]* How so?

HANK: A true God would have never put you in that position. Or have let Satan. Maybe it just seems the Earth has flooded… and no more than the weather is to blame!

NOAH: *[Wiping eyes.]* That makes a little sense. When I heard God speaking to me, I was rather drunk.

HANK: Exactly, you just *think* you heard him speak when in all actuality it was likely delusions brought on by years of excessive alcohol consumption.

EMZARA: I don't like this Noah. Don't discount the Lord!

HANK: Why not? What has he ever done for you and your family?

EMZARA: Oh, you! I wish I had let Noah throw you off when I had the chance! *[Pause.]* The Lord has blessed us in countless ways. He saved us from this awful flood for one!

HANK: No, God caused the flood and it was your husband that saved you. And fine craftsmanship if I don't say so myself.

NOAH: Thank you! It's nice to be appreciated.

HANK: *[Sniffing.]* Did you really put two of every animal in here?

NOAH: Well technically speaking of every clean beast I took by sevens and of beasts that weren't clean I took by two. Of fowls also of the air I took by sevens to *[Begins chuckling.]* keep seed alive upon the face of all the earth!

HANK: *[Laughing.]* You had to be drunk!

NOAH: I have plenty more ale if you care for some!

EMZARA: *[Pleading.]* Noah, don't!

NOAH: Silence, Emzara! I'm tired of suffering! It's time to indulge!

> *[NOAH and HANK get into a barrel of ale; begin stumbling around and acting ridiculous.]*

HANK: I've got your nose!

> *[He pretends to snatch NOAH's nose.]*

NOAH: *[Laughing hysterically.]* I've got yours too!

EMZARA: *[Screaming.]* Noah, think of what the children would say if they saw their father acting out like this!

HANK: They would say he's a good sport, that's what!

> *[He high-fives NOAH.]*

NOAH: Yeah, they would! I'm just glad I found someone who finally understands!

HANK: I feel the same way, brother. While we're at it, why don't we, just for kicks… slaughter all the animals?

NOAH: What, why!?

HANK: You know all this God stuff is bogus. Why are we keeping them here?

NOAH: Well, there isn't really a good reason but killing them seems a little extreme.

HANK: They are simply a part of the larger world, my friend! There's plenty more out there!

NOAH: What will we eat after their meat goes bad?

HANK: We needn't worry about that. The flood will be over any day now. Let's have one gigantic feast in the meantime! Eat all the stores!

NOAH: What about my family?

HANK: They'll enjoy it too! And God doesn't exist so it's not like he'd be angry.

NOAH: Well, I guess I've earned a little fun…

EMZARA: NOAH!

HANK: Ignore her. You more than have. We will slaughter the animals together and *then* make a blood sacrifice of your entire family – TO GOD!

EMZARA: *[At the top of her lungs.]* NO!!

NOAH: The absence of a God doesn't change my love for my family.

HANK: What is love? That's just a myth the world has fed you. Be a true father, husband and end their earthly misery!

EMZARA: Noah, I love you! I truly do! Don't doubt that's real for one second!

HANK: Quiet, woman! Noah is his own man! And you are nothing! You let the whole world die to save your family and they will die too! The sea shows no mercy!

NOAH: *[Stepping forward.]* And neither do I!

HANK: Of course, why else would you send your wife and children to a death devoid of God and afterlife?

NOAH: You're wrong! There is an afterlife, there is a God!

HANK: Then why don't you prove it? God killed all other life and made you watch as it happened!

NOAH: It's easy to accept but that doesn't make it right! God isn't at work against us, or for us. He's inside, guiding us toward light! I made the best choice I could and I know that now. I saved as much life as I was able, and that's more than any others would have tried! So leave! Be gone!

[HANK walks offstage dejectedly.]

EMZARA: *[Embracing NOAH.]* Noah, thank you, thank you! I knew you'd see light.

NOAH: *[Pointing out the window.]* See that arch with the colors? It looks like we we've both seen it.

End of play

TRAIN ROB

CHARACTERS
JOSH MICHAELS: Mousy looking passenger.
SELFISH BASTARD: Middle-aged man in a fashionable coat.
CAMILLE: A woman with faded blonde hair; she has a look suggesting she was once a movie star.
OLD CART LADY: Hunched, grey lady pushing a muffin cart.
CONDUCTOR: Old timey sounding conductor.
GROVER: Tall bandit with face completely covered.
GEOFFREY: Shorter, stocky bandit with face completely covered.

SETTING
A passenger train with seats down either side of the aisle. A cart of muffins and various baked goods is being pushed by an older woman.

PROPS
A cart of muffins (or other baked goods)
A book
A plastic bag
Two guns

[JOSH MICHAELS is walking down the aisle and pauses near a luggage tag with the name Selfish Bastard on it.]

JOSH: Why does it say your name here is selfish bastard?

BASTARD: That's easy, I'm a selfish bastard. I figure a name should represent more than what your parents were thinking at some esoteric moment.

JOSH: So you're selfish… and a bastard?

BASTARD: Of course, I don't attempt to deny or change myself. I'm not some dog waiting for society to give me scraps for sitting pretty.

JOSH: So, I get the philosophy behind it but why that particular name?

BASTARD: I have a family.

JOSH: I don't follow.

BASTARD: I provide for them.

JOSH: So? Sounds selfless if you ask me.

BASTARD: I assure it's you far more selfish than selfless. Did I mention any other families I provide for?

JOSH: You didn't, but surely everyone–

BASTARD: Is just as selfish?

JOSH: Well, yeah!

BASTARD: That's not all though.

JOSH: There's more?

BASTARD: Yes, I gave to charity.

JOSH: Let me guess, it's selfish because you just gave to one.

BASTARD: Yes, I showed favoritism.

JOSH: But less suffer from your choice.

BASTARD: Tell that to the ones that still do.

JOSH: I'll be right back.

BASTARD: I'm sure you will.

> *[JOSH walks to his wife CAMILLE. She has a look to suggest she is wise beyond her years.]*

JOSH: Hun, the strangest of things may have just happened.

CAMILLE: May have? Dear, are you well?

JOSH: Of course, but there's this fellow, who provides for his family, gives to charity, yet is under the delusion that he's selfish.

CAMILLE: And he just happened to confess this state of mind to you?

JOSH: No, that's the thing. I was walking by and noticed his luggage tag said Selfish Bastard.

CAMILLE: He must be really torn up.

JOSH: That's the other thing; he's perfectly okay with it. He thinks I'm the weird one. *[CAMILLE stares matter-of-factly for a minute.]* Care to meet him?

CAMILLE: What? Of course not. He deserves some degree of privacy.

JOSH: Well said, but I'm going back over.

CAMILLE: And you say he's the bastard.

JOSH: No, he says *he's* the bastard and that's what I have to get to the bottom of! *[He leaves CAMILLE, and grabs two muffins from the old woman's cart on his way to BASTARD who is sleeping.]* I came to talk. Thought these might break the ice.

BASTARD: They definitely break something.

JOSH: Oh, hey now, we'll never be friends with that attitude.

BASTARD: That's a shame.

JOSH: By the way do you go to church?

   [Pause.]

BASTARD: Yes and I mourn the futility of faith.

JOSH: Why for God's sake!?

BASTARD: All this praying. We could actually be doing something as a community instead of simply wishing.

JOSH: So then why don't you?

BASTARD: Have you even read my name tag?

JOSH: I don't think I like you.

BASTARD: Well that's worth saying out loud. I don't like cabbage but you don't hear me droning on about it.

JOSH: Maybe you just haven't had it in the proper dish. I entered some coleslaw for the county fair when I was nine and won a ribbon. I could make you some.

69

BASTARD: I really don't think I want to discuss the merits of cabbage with you.

JOSH: See, I try to be your friend and you cast me off. I understand how you feel and all. It's not easy being alone as you obviously are. You may put up a tough front, but you're incredibly transparent. And if it helps, we can, um… hug.

BASTARD: *[Sarcastically.]* That's just what I needed to hear daddy!

[BASTARD embraces him.]

JOSH: Wow, we're really having a breakthrough! I'm going to go tell my wife!

[He runs to CAMILLE.]

CAMILLE: What is it?

JOSH: He cried and hugged me and called me daddy!

CAMILLE: Well, you've rendered me speechless!

JOSH: I think I'll give him some alone time to work through his range of complex emotions.

CAMILLE: Oh no, now I want to meet him. Stay here. *[She walks casually toward BASTARD and sits by him; he is reading a book as if the previous exchange had never happened.]* Hi, you don't know me, but I happened to be married to the man who continues to rudely interrupt you every two minutes.

BASTARD: *[Shaking her hand.]* Charmed.

CAMILLE: I agree with your philosophy.

BASTARD: Do you?

CAMILLE: Yes, it's amazing to think how out of tune the majority of us are with our selfishness.

BASTARD: I've completed various books on the topic.

CAMILLE: *[Intrigued.]* Oh, really? What are their titles?

BASTARD: Well, they aren't books in the literal sense, but I have published them to the air for ears to listen in.

CAMILLE: I think I'd like to have an affair with you.

BASTARD: Right now?

CAMILLE: Is there a better time?

BASTARD: Perhaps when I'm a widower.

CAMILLE: Oh, a selfish bastard with high moral standards?

BASTARD: Well my name is not Dishonest Bastard.

CAMILLE: But isn't it incredibly selfish to just give yourself to one woman?

BASTARD: Ah, but you miss the point of it all. I'm not selfish on purpose, nor do I go out of my way to be so. I, like all others, am just naturally inclined toward it.

CAMILLE: Pity, I could have rocked your world.

BASTARD: Does your husband know you proposition strange men for sex?

CAMILLE: Of course, we have an open marriage.

BASTARD: Now, I must say, I've found a great bit of respect for the old man.

CAMILLE: Why is that?

BASTARD: Well, I myself, am far too selfish to be involved in something so scandalous.

CAMILLE: We're generally unselfish people in comparison to you. You could say Selfish Bastard has met Unselfish Humanitarians.

BASTARD: Interesting. How are you humanitarians?

CAMILLE: My husband hasn't told you, but we give to charity too. Only we donate randomly to a new one each month.

BASTARD: I must admit, you avoid bias that way.

CAMILLE: We also sponsor a family every year.

BASTARD: I get the feeling you're trying to make me look bad, Ms. Camille.

CAMILLE: Not at all, my husband and I just happen to be the exception to your rule of selfishness.

BASTARD: Did you offer your train tickets to anyone else before you got on?

CAMILLE: As a matter of fact I did.

BASTARD: Do what you will now, but I bet when the shades are drawn, and a real crisis approaches, you'll be no less selfish than I am.

[A bang is heard atop the train.]

CAMILLE: I'm going to sit down.

BASTARD: You do that.

[CAMILLE returns to her seat; CONDUCTOR's voice comes over a loud speaker.]

CONDUCTOR: Everyone get seated, there have been minor mechanical malfunctions, but we are working to fix them in a timely manner. Please remain calm.

BASTARD: *[With a wry smile to himself.]* The symbolism will soon meet reality.

[More noises are heard outside the train, with voices; it is clear something more than mechanical issues are afoot.]

CONDUCTOR: Please continue to remain calm. We apologize. There are no mechanical issues. People outside have been spotted breaking into the train. They will be inside any moment. Please cooperate with them, so we may get through the process–

[A struggle is heard over the intercom.]

BASTARD: Any moment now.

[CAMILLE and JOSH slowly make their way toward a back exit in the commotion.

In a swift movement the front door is kicked open; two armed assailants, GROVER and GEOFFREY stand before the passengers. Both have their faces completely covered.]

GROVER: Everyone get out your wallets, and no one be a hero!

BASTARD: Is it okay to be a bastard by chance?

GROVER : You shut your mouth, or you'll get a bullet in it.

BASTARD: I daresay that's a threat. My bowels voiding in the aftermath would be a sore inconvenience for your hostage situation.

GROVER: Shut him up, Geoffrey!

GEOFFREY: Right.

[GEOFFREY walks toward and pistol whips BASTARD; he falls to the floor silently as if planned.]

GROVER: Does anyone else care to join him? No? Then empty your wallets, and put your cash and valuables in the bag.

[A bag is passed around.]

GEOFFREY: Sir, I don't know where the man went.

GROVER: You just knocked him out for Christ sake!

GEOFFREY: Should we search the train?

GROVER: No, this isn't Die Hard and he's not Bruce Willis.

[He spots CAMILLE and JOSHUA crouching by the door ready to jump.]

CAMILLE: We just came to talk with you.

JOSH: Yes, is there anything we can do to help with your, uh, robbery?

GROVER: Geoffrey, kick them out.

GEOFFREY: What, sir?

GROVER: They want off, so let them off.

GEOFFREY: The train is going pretty fast, sir.

GROVER: Did I ask for a flippant observation? No. I said let... them...off!

[Geoffrey grabs CAMILLE and JOSH reluctantly by their shirts and drags them to the front door.]

BASTARD: *[Standing casually by an emergency break.]* I wouldn't do that.

GROVER: And just who the hell do you think you are?

BASTARD: Why, I'm a Bastard, of course!

[BASTARD pulls the emergency break, and sends the assailants, as well as several passengers crashing toward the wall.]

JOSH: *[Getting up.]* Now, that was pretty unselfish!

BASTARD: Saving my own ass? I don't think so.

[He helps up CAMILLE.]

CAMILLE: You were right about us. Self preservation hit us like a ton of bricks.

BASTARD: Like I said: have no illusions, do what comes natural. For good or ill.

JOSH: Can I borrow a pen?

[CAMILLE hands him a pen from her purse.]

JOSH: I think it's time our own luggage tags, say *Return to Mr. and Mrs. Bastard.*

BASTARD: Hey, now, Bastard's my name.

JOSH: What about Blowhard?

BASTARD: It is available!

[All laugh together as lights dim.]

End of play

THE GREAT ARGUMENT

SOCIALISM: Hammer and a sickle. Careful worded, often preachy.
FASCISM: A Nazi Swastika. Paranoid, with a German accent.
CAPITALISM: Uncle Sam in traditional flag garb. Arrogant, dismissive toward others.
MONARCHY: A Crown. Extremely vain, *she* has little tolerance for dissent.

SETTING
A blank, white space reminiscent of heaven, possibly purgatory.

PROPS
Four Swords
Two small rifles
Two larger rifles

[CAPITALISM, SOCIALISM, FASCISM, MONARCHY are all engaged in a heated debate.]

SOCIALISM: My system is by far the fairest, comrades! The proletariat does the work, therefore they deserve the power!

CAPITALISM: It can't work, it's against human nature!

SOCIALISM: Humans are naturally communal. You would have us devolve to lesser primates!

FASCISM: *Mein freunden*, don't fight amongst yourselves. The real enemies are those we can't see – those hiding, plotting. We must weed them out and then enjoy a true utopia!

CAPITALISM: I kind of like his idea –

SOCIALISM: *[Interrupting.]* Capitalism!

CAPITALISM: Sorry. It's my last stage.

MONARCHY: You are all gravely mistaken. God put me on this earth so that I might rule!

SOCIALISM: What God?

CAPITALISM: Socialism, don't be like *that*!

FASCISM: A good religion is subordinate to the interests of the state.

MONARCHY: And the state is me!

FASCISM: You shall join me then! Or perish!

MONARCHY: The crown answers to no one but God, and God appointed me, therefore I must only listen to myself!

FASCISM: Prepare for war!

[FASCISM draws a sword.]

SOCIALISM: This is not in the interest of the proletariat! You're only feeding the industrial machine that turns soldiers into cannon fodder!

CAPITALISM: But, on the other end, there's opportunity...

SOCIALISM: Capitalism, that is low, even by your standards!

CAPITALISM: Well if war is inevitable why should everyone be losers?

MONARCHY: Exactly. You shall supply my war effort!

CAPITALISM: With pleasure.

FASCISM: Who will supply my own? Socialism? I know we've had our differences and I've sought quite often to annihilate you completely but, I need your help. What do you say?

SOCIALISM: All right. I will sell you metals and oil. *[FASCISM draws own sword and proceeds to fight MONARCHY.]* Go, Fascism! Kill!

CAPITALISM: Come on Monarchy, you can do it!

[FASCISM gains the advantage.]

SOCIALISM: Yes! Pin him down!

CAPITALISM: Get up you lazy Monarchy! *[MONARCHY gets up and stabs FASCISM in the chest.]* Finally! Sweet victory at last.

SOCIALISM: Damn, it looks I've made a somber investment. *[FASCISM falls on MONARCHY with their sword, stabbing them dead as well.]* Or not.

CAPITALISM: What do we do now?

SOCIALISM: Well we were at peace. But I've kind of convinced everyone you're evil by now.

CAPITALISM: Same here.

[CAPITALISM draws sword.]

SOCIALISM: Oh, please, a sword?

[SOCIALISM draws gun.]

CAPITALISM: I need a moment.

[Exit CAPITALISM.]

SOCIALISM: Take all the time you want. The world will see my value as you wait.

[Renter CAPITALISM after a minute or two.]

CAPITALISM: I got it!

[CAPITALISM draws bigger gun.]

SOCIALISM: The proletariat will not fail!

[SOCIALISM runs in the other direction firing gun.]

CAPITALISM: What was that for?

SOCIALISM: I was defending my cause over... *[Points.]* There!

CAPITALISM: Then I shall defend my own over... *[Points in opposite direction.]* There!

SOCIALISM: This is ridiculous. Why not just fight each other openly and get things done with once and for all?

CAPITALISM: No. That can't happen. Our guns are too equal in size. It could endanger lives but more importantly, profits. What we must do instead is have others fight *for us* in an endless series of proxy wars to determine the victor!

SOCIALISM: Won't that take a long time?

CAPITALISM: Forty, fifty years, tops.

SOCIALISM: And after that we're done with war? The proletariat can go back to peaceful living unencumbered by the vicious machine that seeks to kill them for its own gain?

CAPITALISM: Well... the loser will endure significant economic fallout, and the winner will secure its place in the world by unnecessary incursion into other nations in an attempt to reinforce its dominance.

SOCIALISM: Can't there just be peace?

CAPITALISM: What would I tell the defense industry? A lot of jobs are at stake. Trust me, brutal proxy wars are the best alternative to unemployment.

SOCIALISM: I don't know. I think we can just let the different governments decide which ideology is best. Blood is not productive.

CAPITALISM: Don't make me land on the moon. I'll do it!

SOCIALISM: But, what? I don't understand.

CAPITALISM: Sputnik, space. I see what you're up to. Bombing us.

SOCIALISM: We were simply advancing mankind and showing what an empowered workforce can accomplish!

CAPITALISM: No, you're going to bomb us. I can feel it.

SOCIALISM: Evidence?

CAPITALISM: Eastern Europe.

SOCIALISM: And you don't see how that's securing our borders after two vicious wars?

CAPITALISM: I could but I don't. To the moon!

SOCIALISM: You do that. I'm going to support Ho Chi Minh and the Viet Cong.

CAPITALISM: What!?

SOCIALISM: Yeah, I think it's what everyone is looking for; an end to exploitation and imperialism from other nations through a strong, central government.

CAPITALISM: Well, we certainly can't have that. The market must speak for the Vietnamese.

SOCIALISM: But the market has thrown it into poverty and chaos!

CAPITALISM: Temporarily. It's just in a transition state.

SOCIALISM: For hundreds of years?

CAPITALISM: Perhaps.

SOCIALISM: Do what you want. I'm going to give weapons to the Viet Cong.

CAPITALISM: And I will oppose you and make up my own government, pretending like it's always been there.

SOCIALISM: What sorry sap could you possibly get to lead such a farce?

CAPITALISM: There's this guy, Diem. Real straight shooter, Roman Catholic. Strong choice considering the Buddhist majority.

SOCIALISM: I don't think the people will take that so well.

CAPITALISM: You're right. I'll assassinate him.

SOCIALISM: That was sudden.

CAPITALISM: Eh, I've got a civil rights thing to fix.

SOCIALISM: But that doesn't end the war.

CAPITALISM: It doesn't? Won't the Vietnamese suddenly support us now that we've killed the tyrant we put in place? We've seen the error of our ways.

SOCIALISM: It's hard to say that when you're still bombing the snot out of an entire population.

CAPITALISM: Good point. I'll just kill a hundred or so thousand more civilians and be done with it. I'm sure they'll forgive us in the long run.

SOCIALISM: That's a terrible way to look at things.

CAPITALISM: Kennan loved his dominoes, what can I say?

SOCIALISM: Well, now that that's over, let's enjoy some games together.

CAPITALISM: What do you have in mind?

SOCIALISM: Swimming, track, all that jazz.

CAPITALISM: I would but you're kind of in Afghanistan.

SOCIALISM: So?

CAPITALISM: I have to boycott you.

SOCIALISM: Well fine, then I'll boycott you later.

CAPITALISM: Good.

SOCIALISM: Great.

CAPITALISM: And I'll build lasers in space.

SOCIALISM: Wait, what?

CAPITALISM: I'm building lasers in space. Maybe you won't piss me off next time.

SOCIALISM: Damn. I would love to match you on the space laser front, but I'm kind of bogged down in Afghanistan.

CAPITALISM: *[Laughing.]* You're such a basket case, Socialism. That will never happen to me.

SOCIALISM: Can I borrow some plaster or something?

CAPITALISM: Why?

SOCIALISM: My wall's falling apart.

CAPITALISM: Sorry man, Reagan said tear it down.

SOCIALISM: That's cold.

> *[Coughs.]*

CAPITALISM: Are you going to be all right, Socialism?

SOCIALISM: I don't think so. The doctor said I've only got a few more years at the most.

CAPITALISM: Oh, man, that sucks. We've practically been married these past forty years.

SOCIALISM: Remember the time I didn't give food to the residents of East Berlin? And you airlifted it in?

CAPITALISM: Our honeymoon. How could I forget?

SOCIALISM: It's been a long journey full of ups and downs but a lot of good memories.

CAPITALISM: I remember the first time I saw you.

SOCIALISM: You do?

CAPITALISM: It was right after the Russian Revolution. I was one of the countries invading and even then you looked ravishing.

SOCIALISM: Oh, Capitalism. You charmer!

CAPITALISM: Shall we make love one last time?

[They begin kissing.]

SOCIALISM: Oh, yes, send your ship in my free market!

CAPITALISM: Fill me up with your Obamacare!

End of play

HEAVEN OF OZ

CHARACTERS

JUDY GARLAND: Insecure about her appearance and abilities. Bears great guilt for having died and left her children.

RAY BOLGER: A bit full of himself. Has seen others suffering but endeared little himself. Confident in his acting and stage abilities. Feels beloved and antagonistic to those professing otherwise.

BERT LAHR: Melancholy. Successes often marred by personal failures. Still humorous but somehow it seems forced. He was the first of the four to die and cannot help but put some blame on those that lived a little longer.

JACK HALEY: A gruff voice in contrast to his role as Tin Man. Hardened personality with an air of understanding.

SETTING

The magical poppy field from the Wizard of Oz film. A Yellow Brick Road winds off into the distance.

[RAY BOLGER is walking up a yellow brick road toward a poppy field where JUDY GARLAND, BERT LAHR, and JACK HALEY are standing.]

BERT: You sure were a long time coming.

RAY: I had to stop and visit Margaret Hamilton.

BERT: The Wicked Witch!?

RAY: Stop it! She was a very nice lady. Great with kids! Now, where's Judy?

JUDY: Ray!

[She hugs RAY.]

JACK: Do I get a hug too or do you really miss him most, after all?

[JUDY half-smiles and hugs JACK.]

JUDY: What did you think of my Liza, Ray? I saw you working with her for a time.

RAY: She was delightful to the end. Reminded me so much of you.

JUDY: *[Blushing.]* Ray, Ray, Ray... such a charmer, even in death!

JACK: I'd be a charmer too. If the Wizard had given me a better heart!

JUDY: Jack, I was so sad to hear about your attack. Your son was married to Liza for a time. It's a shame it couldn't have lasted. She's had so many husbands...

BERT: *[Feeling left out.]* Does anyone care to sing a song?

JUDY: I suppose it couldn't hurt. Which one?

RAY: "Ain't She Sweet?" I sang it while I danced with Verna Felton!

BERT: I was thinking one we'd actually sung *together*.

JACK: "We're Off To See The Wizard?"

BERT: Of course, I love that one!

JUDY: Me too!

RAY: *[Rolling eyes.]* Me three!

> *[They all link arms.]*

JACK: On the count of three; one, two –

RAY: Owe! Bert pinched me!

JACK: Bert, why did you pinch Ray?

BERT: Sure, take his side! If you're planning a witch hunt you best go after the one who's actually friends with the witch!

RAY: I told you she's a nice lady!

BERT: Yeah, right. Go… dance for Dr. Pepper!

RAY: Someone sounds jealous.

BERT: Making a fool of myself on national television? Not up my alley!

JUDY: You two stop it! We were all friends once, remember?

RAY: *[Leering at BERT.]* Vividly.

JACK: How about we give something else a try? We could act out the scene from the Witch's castle!

JUDY: *[Trailing off.]* Oh, no, not that one. Brings back too many memories…

JACK: All right, there's plenty of other scenes. Any preference?

RAY: Do we have to do ones from Oz? There were so many other highpoints in my career!

BERT: Yeah, in yours. Not all of us were so lucky after.

JACK: That is true Ray.

RAY: Fine, we'll do more from Oz.

JUDY: How about the one where I go home? I've never really felt at home.

BERT: That sounds fine to me, Judy.

JUDY: Too bad Billie's not here. It might have been possible.

RAY: Where is Billie by the way?

JUDY: Oh, I think she's watching over her grandchildren at the moment. I spoke with her not long ago.

BERT: See Ray, she talks to the *good* witch!

RAY: *[Mockingly.]* Whatever you say, Snagglepuss!

BERT: What!?

RAY: Snagglepuss, the cartoon character? Hanna-Barbera based him off you. He always wound up back where he started or worse off than he was before. Fitting analogy I thought.

BERT: I'll have you know, I was the only character in the Wizard of Oz with *two* solo numbers!

RAY: But the audience still walked out of *Waiting for Godot*.

BERT: That's unrelated... and it was eventually successful...and I won the Tony!

RAY: For Foxy.

BERT: I don't know why I let you bring me down. I didn't accomplish quite as much as you but I still won best Shakespearean actor of the year!

RAY: *[Yawning.]* Boring.

BERT: I suppose you thought Toby Noe was the best role ever!

RAY: He wasn't the most noble of characters, but a good show of my range.

BERT: Sure. You were a brainless mooch; no different from Oz! And life!

    [RAY advances toward BERT.]

JACK: Come on guys, this has gone on long enough! *[Exit JUDY.]* You made Judy leave!

BERT: Yeah, Ray, look what you did!

RAY: Me!? I was her favorite!

BERT: So it finally comes out.

RAY: I didn't mean it like *that*.

JACK: How did you mean it Ray?

RAY: She liked you too Jack.

JACK: Yet she missed you most of all. I never quite got over that.

RAY: So you're jealous too?

JACK: No, just disillusioned. You were always most important to Judy. And yet, you got here last.

RAY: What does that mean?

JACK: Think about it. Who picked up the pieces all these years? Frank? He's still too busy getting drunk! And God knows Bert was no help.

BERT: Hey, I did my part. I was here before you!

JACK: Were you? It didn't seem like it!

BERT: I was the first to go. I knew what it felt like to be alone without your loved ones. And I can honestly say I've made Judy smile more than any of you!

RAY: Guys, maybe we shouldn't be arguing. I think she still needs us.

BERT: Yeah, look at her over there crying. Poor thing. Let's go cheer her up.

JACK: Remember now, let's all get along. The last thing she needs is more fighting.

> [JUDY reenters, JACK, BERT and RAY run up and embrace her.]

JUDY: This was unexpected…

JACK: We just wanted to show you how much we still care Judy.

JUDY: [Chuckling.] I think you've succeeded!

BERT: Do you want to come back and reminisce some more with us? I promise, only happy memories!

JACK: Like the time we stood up to that humbug wizard!

JUDY: Oh, come on now, Frank wasn't *that* bad. He just liked a shot every now and then.

RAY: Remember the time his briefcase was leaking?

BERT: *[Laughing.]* Yeah, it turned out there was a bottle of whisky in it, and he'd left the cap off!

JACK: It was funny… until Victor made me clean it up. When I was Hickory, he treated me like Hickory! Practically threw me on the woodpile!

BERT: Ah, now *this* is like old times!

RAY: Let's try singing that song again, fellas! Are you in Judy?

JUDY: No, I think I'll stay here and watch my daughter for a while. She's the most beautiful woman in the world no matter what anyone might say.

BERT: All right Judy.

   [He kisses her head and exits with RAY and JACK.]

JUDY: What's heaven without pills? *[She looks into the distance.]* Can't wait to see you again my darling Liza. But for God sakes, take more time than I did.

End of play

About the Author...

Ben Ditmars was first published in his college publication. Since then he has been featured in several online literary journals. He has also recorded several episodes of a podcast on poetry (Lyrical Versification) with his cohost, Amber Jerome~Norrgard. Listen in on iTunes or Stitcher Radio. Currently, Ben lives in Marion, Ohio where he works in childcare. He loves historical documentaries and all things gnome.

Find him on:

Twitter: @benditty
Facebook Page: facebook.com/benjaminditmars
Blog: benjaminditmars.wordpress.com

Made in United States
North Haven, CT
23 June 2025

70044211R00055